# OLD WORLD, NEW WORLD

*poems by*

## DAVID HOLBROOK

**Rapp & Whiting** London

## ACKNOWLEDGEMENTS

Some of these poems have been published in the following journals and the author is grateful to the editors for permission to reproduce them here: *Twentieth Century, London Magazine, Harper's Bazaar, Critical Quarterly, Poetry Review, New Statesman, The Listener, Cambridge Review, The Times Literary Supplement, Chirino* (Rhodesia), *Workshop, Blackwood's Magazine* and *The Use of English.*

'Bowling for A Pig', was also published in the author's *Children's Writing* (Cambridge University Press, 1967).

SBN 85391 144 4

© 1969 DAVID HOLBROOK
FIRST PUBLISHED IN 1969 BY
RAPP AND WHITING LIMITED
76 NEW OXFORD STREET LONDON WC1
PRINTED IN GREAT BRITAIN BY
WILLIAM LEWIS (PRINTERS) LIMITED CARDIFF

# CONTENTS

## STEP

My father, whom I love, has had another son,
Thirty-eight years after his first: and on the telephone
The sixty-one-year-old sounded so happy. 'What!'
I cried, 'and did you bath it — you?' 'Oh God not
Me, boy, no, I daren't, no!' And I remember how he wrote
Once in his diary of my baby fingers, and about
His amazement, that a creature should appear so perfect, small,
Out of a woman's body in so little time, so little time at all.

I turn and tell my wife: but sense another one
Who'd like to know. I want to say, 'Your prophecy's begun
Now to fulfil itself — as you said, after your death
He has another wife, and children!' — and then hear her breath
Sighed in a knowing 'Ah!' and laughter at the quaint
Boyish energy of the man she loved. I feel that if I went
Somewhere I could tell her, that the suffering brown eyes
Would come out of their coma for her son, even express surprise . . .

But then I'm lost, and for a moment stand inert
In the old way, as when, dying and dead, she took my heart
Down to the subsoil where the stumbling priest, that autumn day,
Recited to our tears and she was lowered far away —
She on whose breast I sobbed, she whose piano melody
Thrilled on my child's nerves in that long Eden holiday
Between birth and the gradual separation till the grave ropes creak,
And bitter apprehension of implacable truths come break
In great sobs as the shovels heave the earth back on the box.

No time at all. And then the instant passed, and the long grassy mound
Passed with its weedy strangle from my mind.
Another mother, other sons: so little time at all:
Bewildered thus we turn from cradle-frill to pall.
My eldest daughter's nubile now, before my love and I
Begin to learn to love. Only the other day
After his last good lunch old Walter fell away
Tidily, after four neat score years. Colleagues in their prime
Go in the chance futility of human life in Time.

I swallow, breathe again. Hear my wife's puzzled call:
'Is everything all right?' 'Yes, flourishing!' So little time! So little time at all!

## BOWLING FOR A PIG

One of the first things we did when we came to this village
Was to visit a Fete in the Rectory Garden,
And there were some kale-pots, with numbers and large holes
Into which you threw tennis-balls; and nearby in a crate,
Like a shivering maiden chained to a rock
(Except that she wasn't shivering, but scratching herself daintily)
Was a piglet, in a long crate, strawed and bristly,
Rubbing her silver-haired flank on the silver-haired wood.

I bowled for this pig, determined to show the village
I was no town fool unskilled in the hand.
Two and sixpence I spent, raising my score to thirty,
And the piglet was mine. We cleared out a stable –
Sharp irons, unstable log-piles and rusty bicycles
Replaced by a golden thicket of crackling straw.
Then we heaved in the piglet, who snuffed, squealed, and buried.
And then, just as we thought she had died from mishandling
Or fright, dashed at us, sallying and veering away,
Just like a dog, teasing its master, to express affection.

'Henrietta' we called her, after a gentleman friend,
And Henry was pleased, and the piglet was pleased to be called
Something. She ate washing, the sleeves of shirts, or apron-
Strings that dangled. Our paddock, a mass of nettles,
Mallows and kecks of all kinds, rubble, and granular
Long-rotted, muck-filled earth – this she rooted,
Driving up tunnels and earthworks, wallows and simple snuffs
From which with a 'hough!' she emerged to scamper two circuits,
Lapping the barn at a good fifteen miles an hour: then tease us,
Pretending to eat a shirt, or actually eat a shirt,
Or drag a petticoat like a ring-trophy through the mud.

And then – the meal she consumed! At first small packets,
But then this mournful pig became hollow and wobbly-flanked,
And I had to buy sacks, huge fat unmanageable hundredweights,
Which stood bulky and gross beside a smallish gilt pig,
Which later stood bulky and gross beside a smallish sad sack,
And the bills mounted. But we planned to breed,
To give Henrietta the happiness other elephantine sows
Screamed about in the night on the other side of our lane,
As part of the landscape mounted another part,
Breeding another litter: she must have that,
And dozens of Henries and Herberts and Harries would squeal
Round our snout-ridged paddock. Then we thought of the cost of the meal,
Christmas came, autumn bills, the seasons of greed, and . . . hams
And goodwill. Then, after one bad post, I rang
The bacon works, and for a lorry. That day I left
The house by a seldom-used door, not near the paddock;
My wife hurried in and out, as people do
When someone within is grievously sick or dead – not even
Retrieving a couple of dishclothes Henrietta wound
Tastefully round her neck, then buried, then rooted and ate,
While we watched her with craven eyes, too guilty to speak.

Since autumn I'd thrown her heaps of windfalls to eat,
Red, tempting and succulent: these she'd delightedly sniff,
Hough, gamble, and toss. She loved them, and frosty days
Had been happy for both of us, winner and munching pig
Under pale blue autumn skies. Those apple baits
I employed to lure Henrietta up the ramp. One last ear toss,
A clatter of bolts, 'sign 'ere sir', and off she went,
While we gloomily ate, and hadn't the heart to confess

The misery hanging over us. What, you say, just for a pig?
Yet I've seen farmers sorrowful, at the loss of a horse,
Or even a handsome bullock. Sad at necessity.
But Henrietta! For the Christmas bills! Betraying
The prize that made my shirts armless, companion
To my small scratch-back girls? It cast a light
On human weakness. We could do this! No trust
Should rest on such as we were.

                                  She made good:
Grade A in all her parts — a paper
Came in a day or two. We thought of our pig lingering
In the steel pens, no clunch to root, no washing,
No mallow flowers, no chase with angry wife,
No scratch-back children! Only the forced cake-walk,
Into some cold machine. The stun. The hook. The knife.
And then the needle-pickled bacon, clean long sides and hams
Divided and eaten throughout suburbia. Twenty-two pounds ten
Was all I had. It went. Some of it even on bacon.
She would have got too big, we rationalised. The meal
Would have cost too much for us. Yet we felt her sacrificed
To an improvidence that wrecks so many plans,
Ineffectual and sad. We were in that steel pen
With our young maiden pig.

                                How I'd love now to feel
The morning winner's pleasure of hearing her lot squeal,
Dashing under the straw as the half-door opens — pail
Clattering (her tenth litter!), slops and swills,
Grateful old mother sow!

                        Alas!
Even her carcase ticket's burned now with the settled bills!

## NEW WORLD

The Atlantic, pink, grey and humid: early,
Very early, at first light. The ship swashes on.
We are tired of this desert of unpredictable sea.
Suddenly, a pink finger; a short pink stumpy finger —
Then another. Whatever can it be? They build up:
As the dawn light grows, Manhattan rises out of the swamp.
What a strange sight! No trees, land, mountains:
Pink, man-made towers, nearly as many as in San Gimigniano.

Then the pilot jumping on board in black oilskins,
Buoys, dark streams of smoke behind air liners,
Freighters, wharves, the derelict longshores,
Prisons, forts, and the suspension roadways
We seem to slide under only by inches.

After that, much like the back-end of anywhere.
I went down in the cabin for you, fretful baby,
Nursing the vision of the few small fingers
Rising over the edge.

                              It is now a year later:
When we left, we did not even watch the skyscrapers
Disappear back into the seaboard storms.
Three new words a day, but you still talk nonsense.
I catch on your face the crumpled frown
With which you looked at the fingers of the New World.

Yet there was even a time before that.
Your pink face blued briefly by a shadow —
There is your shut expression, thrusting out of her womb!

In vain I try to imagine the world before you commented on it!

# ELDORADO

The American summer is a long stretch of superheated madness:
White mid-Western light silvers huge heaps of cars:
In Massachussetts I saw a whole mountain of orange and blue school buses.

I step from a car on a rainy campus morning:
Tornado touchdowns have been reported a few miles West.
Ought I to go and shelter my family in the basement?
Will the granite Mail Office soar into a whirlwind
Before I have stuck my damp pepperminty Washingtons?
Shall I go home and take my family to a fallout shelter?

A visiting lecturer in a crumpled white jacket
I ended my Transatlantic journey dazed with Chianti;
Taking turns with the baby's bottle on the 'City of Miami'
Wow-wowing across the dark green boring prairie:
Acres of maize and soya dotted with silos like cigar cases.

The baby has been my salvation:
The only one of the July-cursing family
To sleep through the windstorm that came tearing the trees in the small hours
Like a hostile Army out of a clear Illinois night.
He complains only moderately of the melting heat
While our brains seethe and boil with dissociation,
As we lie pouring sweat to the dervish trills of cicadas.

One afternoon, in Chicago, as I sniffed him
Holding his face to mine, a negro father's face softened:
Yet through his downy hair I could see, on the horizon
Black smoke rolling skyscraper-high over the West Side.

11

Last night a race riot over unscrewed fire hydrants,
A black youth shot for it: today the wire shutters are up.
Yet here we are — the only white family on this lake beach,
Scampering on the grubby sand scattered with heat-killed fish,
Which last night's electric storm has done nothing to clear.
Yet the black face softened, as a white father hides his madness
Behind his child's open-mouthed, hungry-eyed stare.
I suppose he could see I was giving way to unAmerican anxiety:
'The Mettle of Americans' a great theme of the *Chicago Tribune*,
Commending their latest demonstrations of sanity
Such as bombing neutral zones. NAB MASS MURDERER:
BARBAROUS INJURIES: NO EVIDENCE OF ABNORMALITY!
That's the headlines for today, folks.


In Urbana Champaign, those dynamic twin cities
July put the fear of God's Country into me too, from the antics of the fezzed Shriners,
To the long white Minuteman, followed by one crazy old lady
Dressed in gauze wings, representing only her slippered self
('She jes' marches every year' — the Only Survivor?).
From the sexy net tights on the Dance School child majorette,
From the lorryload of American Mothers of World War II,
('Proudly they gave their sons', the horrible old bitches),
From the negro goody-goody clubs in stigmatic gold and purple,
From the white-horned military bands, and above all from Reverend Taps —
Bloody echoing bugles while some wretched bloody serviceman
Lowered the bloody flag; while a Wesleyan preacher
Wetted electronically about the need for 'subordination'.
Infant son saw it all, except the fireworks, which we correctly anticipated as too violent,
And the set pieces too prophetic, from Batman to a naval broadside,

12

In which everything went down at the end, as indeed it will
Unless something radical happens to America —
Like that negro father's face softening as he saw me smelling my baby.
He dare do that, as his sons dare flirt with my daughter
In the green waves of Lake Michigan, while only a few blocks away
Our sort were bloodying his sort for no good reason.


Most of what I saw of the Land of Opportunity
I saw through the downy film of my child's first hair:
The silly strings of nite-lites, Dog'n'Suds bars,
The spotty tarts and the old man fumbling in garbage cans,
The wallowing cadillacs and the derelict railways,
The thousands of miles of man-spoiled landscape:
Fat students in bummy Bermudas and frayed jean cut-offs
Reading John Stuart Mill with cribs in the cafeteria;
The cracked concrete roads, the strange combination of indifference and kindliness,
The stench of bad sewers, and the ineffectualness of all public services . . .

Six months and I have our own estimation of Eldorado!

## OLDE WORLDE

On the Lebanon Road out of Hanover,
Anglicised campus town in New England,
Down by the Mink Brook, a red brick house,
A collapsing verandah, the white paint peeling,
Ill-fitting sashes, squashes and corn in the garden:
There we stayed until the end of summer.
A signed photograph of Robert Frost in the parlour
Hung above a complete set of the *Oxford English Dictionary*.
An oppossum in the log-pile, while at night
A plumy skunk came to root about in the garbage.

We played through the Professor's wife's folksong collection,
On her flat Broadwood, full of the debris of flower-arrangements;
Rocked homesick English dons in the rickety chairs,
Ate small black slimy tough Concord grapes, boiled squashes.
It could have been taken as genuine homespun:
There was even some real bread about — at a dollar a loaf.

Yet behind the scenes — what dissociation!
Behind all the New Hampshire folk-weave,
How the stormwater dripped through the old academic's meanness!
How the fly-screens trapped one's fingers,
The homespun beds, board hard, screeched and collapsed!
So filthy the rag rugs they had to be laundromatted
At which they did undo themselves. At great expense
We never made love in that house for the whole two months.
We fought once, pushing one another against the execrable lumber
Round and round the bedroom shuffling our feet in the clobber.

At night we rocked the shaky cot to the stringy August lightning,
Or to the hullabaloo of next-door teenage parties.
One day, to mend ourselves, we took out a canoe:
The Brook smelt so badly of oil it made us sick.
Round a corner we came to a missile silo, stolidly smoking.

On our return, fah-do sirens, pulsating red lights,
Pumps roaring like the Blitz: oilskinned men collecting
For the Hanover fireman's ball. That night the skunk
Met the old mongrel from next door over some king-crab legs.
We had to stuff the frames with the air-mail *Times*
Till skunk seemed preferable to the wood-smoke within.

Oh, that house was a great taste of the poetic side of America.
I yearned for Chicago, where once we made love
After a steak supper during a tornedic storm,
Even while still stunned by the indescribable squalor of 63rd Street.

# SECOND AVENUE TO COW LANE

Had he been there, I would have told him
About the English muffins in the bar on Second Avenue,
How good the coffee was, and the buttered eggs.
Police cadets came in, wearing revolvers.

It was one of the few places over there we felt at home in,
Not because of the silent young cops, but because how glad the woman was,
To serve good coffee, drawing up iced water with it,
Wiping down the spick and span counter, and smiling genuine.

He's gone, so we can't tell him: we've been all that way since.
His calf-yards are empty, dung cleared down to the clunch,
And in them grow tall weeds, with sumptuous yellow flowers.

Walking round the corner to lean on his fences
Was like walking round Gramercy Park to the breakfast counter:
Harry with his great nose, like the woman, proud in her place,
Lighting up all around her, glad to talk when you came along.

I can't tell him, and how does it matter?
She'll follow Harry into oblivion after a thousand breakfasts,
Across there at the other end of the Gulf Stream:
He's more remote. The tallest yellow weed in his yard
Stands gay like a thistle I painted once in a foreground
That thrilled me, as I held its golden points in paint.
The growth in the dead stockman's dead yard
Seems to lunge at me: the weariness of clearing them now!

What will become of them? I walk back through my uncut grass
Heavy with summer dew: I could be walking back
From the bar on Second Avenue. About the same distance:
The same soil underneath, waiting to claim us all.

# HYDE PARK

*For Arthur and Virginia Heisermann*

Brace your prickling self to get in the cab:
It billows heat, like a brick-oven.
Rivulets in his hair, the sagging cabman
Laconics 'Twenny-one' into his hand-mike:
'Twenny-one' crackles back heat-wracked control,
'Six-eleven Wes' Illinois.' In Fifth Street
The Commercial Bank fairlights thermometer figures out a hundred.

Six-eleven is 'home'. You and the children sitting
Round the hired air conditioner in the window.
The weather-boarded little box smells of hot planks.
We have stopped thinking and moving. At midday
White blinding light from a pale slate-grey sky
Growls on the suburban grids of streets: the trees go limp.
The cicadas wind like maniac cracker whistles.

The exhaled humidity of the ocean of maize and soya
Drowns the town at night: we lie slimy with sweat.
Beyond the neonlit shack bars, threading through the Prairie
Freight trains smash their bells and sough. Our baby
Rashed with ammonia, thirsty, moans and thrashes.
The hottest mid-West Summer for thirty-five years
In Champaign-Urbana twin small-towns. All night I search in my dreams
For a scrap of paper: an address someone gave us:
A professor in Chicago: 'Call on them — they're nice people.'

A hundred and fifty miles away the nearest breeze
Blows through my unsleeping dreams across Lake Michigan.

I didn't know what to make of his nervous laugh:
'Sure, you come and stay,' he said, 'We can picnic and swim in the lake'.
You understand — these people had never heard of us:
I wish I had never said anything bad about America.

More furnace cabs! Mistakes over mid-West time!
How we fought our way in hot cars up the old I.C.!
How Sixty-third Street smelt under the crashing Elevated
Straddling the melting junk-strewn street!

Now close your eyes: and open them on a promontory.
We are seated on wiry grass, with a cool wind in our hair.
Red smoke rolls far away inland from the steelworks side.
We are by a coastguard station with masts. Behind sparkles the Marina,
And, beyond, down-town skyscrapers galaxy the Lake Shore.
Negro youths from Blackstone play chase-me-charlie among the scraps of litter.
Our friends open a basket of French bread, chicken casserole and Chianti.
We bathe in the green Michigan among white cubes of rock.
The embankment is called Hyde Park and is rather like Hyde Park.

In a cot with the lake breeze sweet on his face
Our baby sleeps his first deep sleep for a fortnight:
We and the children and the American family
Pad around like wet dogs and gnash into watermelon.

That pleasant trickle of random thoughts of the temperate climate
Starts up again. We began to relate, other than in snarls.
How good to remember what is good about life!
You can even sit outside! The environment can be genial!
It was like a hillside in Siena on a spring day,
Like April by the Serpentine, like the Bois de Boulogne in May,
Or September at home, with the mists and earliest apples.

Later, indoors, as a black storm ravaged the Lake shores
We talked about books and education and Europe
While their children and ours slept beside generous fans
In their lofty Victorian house, cool, solid and English.
They made us love Chicago as much as they did,
From the condenser-like Merino Towers to the deepest hellish car-park,
Every meat-yard and smelting and ghetto of it.
It was like the Blitz: if you were alive you were alive,
And belonged to the human circuit, even on the Six-lane Lakeshore Drive.

I still feel a bit of me belongs to Blackstone,
Where we came alive again in that Michigan breeze,
By that touch of amazing American generosity!

# A DAY OFF IN OXFORD

Huge yellow stone heads on the Sheldonian Theatre
Fascinate you all the day.
Faces worn flat by time. We pass them again.
'I don't want to grow old, David.' In a bookshop
A whole pit full of Theology and Psychology.
Tired, we sit at a green park table in a college garden.
Then Sung and T'ang ceramics, blue dynasty scarabs,
Pre-Dynasty, prehistory, sherds and relics.
A scrap of fine dark hair in a gritty burial urn.
Upstairs we exclaim at a terracotta Medici, then bolt.

Slim beside me your knife presses blood from your steak.
I shift along so that I can press your side.
I hear our talk coming, so many assumptions behind it,
As excited as if we had only recently met,
But pauses that long could only be tolerated
By those who have been married for nearly twenty years.

When our ices arrive your weaning disquiet arises.
There you are, imitating the baby: 'Choc-lick!'
His argot in his absence panics us.
Making some excuse, we down our coffee too hot.
He is Oxford stone crumbled by acid rain:
He is bruised by the traffic roar: the fah-do
Of an ambulance is for him: he lies pale on his pyre;
Sodom and Gomorrah burn under the cliff where his tent is pitched:
Lorenzo has poisoned him: he is being eaten by an aborigine.

Incidentally, I am very much in love with you:
The way you gestured with your umbrella at things
Made me want to bite into the soft hair at the back of your neck.
We'll come back to that later. I must drive you home
In alarm in case your fair baby with a blue stare
Will never be able to reconstitute his mother
Who has dared to take one day off with her husband.

# WRAPPED UP

So, we begin to emerge from the caul!
He had to wind us within it, to find himself
Where there was nothing to find: we had to begin him.
Or rather, you did. Without you he would be nobody:
You had to take that risk!
I've only been playing with fire.
For you it is as grave as an insane journey
This mothering dissolution of yourself.
I've had to live with scraps of a not-you.

Now he's no longer otherworldly: the danger lessens.
He has resources of his own, except for lapses.
At three-quarters he no longer has that crazy beauty
That entrances one out of oneself,
So that one wishes the world would pass away:
If only one could go, smokily involved within one's baby,
Become that quivering soft bud of love,
Eat one another!

No wonder you've been depressed!
The house has been shrieking with cannibalism:
He wants to eat us all,
And really has to — that's how he becomes himself.
Here we are on the floor with him, bears or tigers:
Symbols of what for nine months we have been —
Voracity itself, no symbols, but the very jaws.

'They're so wrapped up in their baby', people say.
He and I, however, are now becoming disillusioned.
Our wills clash: I find him more sticky than soulful.
There are aspects of his personality which are tiresome.
I wish he would grow up. And he in his turn wishes
I could grow up enough not to be involved
In the raving paranoia of his teething nights.

So, our honeymoon is over. We are licking our lips and wounds.
I have been glad to have been consumed.
I am glad to have taken every fragment of him inside myself,
And he is glad to have taken what he can out of me!

No wonder the Aborigines have secret baby-feasts!

# WHIPSNADE

African Larynx, coming out of a hawthorn bush:
I hold my baby like a lifebelt.

I could easily throw him to the Kodiak bears.

Two feet from a tiger's puzzled mask, he makes
His love-noise appropriate for Pussy: my nape hair bristles.
Why does the dead-pan Polar bear, like a ridge of snow-rug,
Pendulum his great head into the wind, on those massive claw-props?
He is like an ice-berg shaking its grey head:
Silently we retreat with the Arctic metronome in our blood.

What does baby think? I remember Tolstoy
With his head in the bear's mouth, the teeth razoring.
Tom is as puzzled as I am by the enigmatic muzzles,
I can tell that: neither his soft, 'Ah!' nor his angry 'No!'
Generate a flicker over the Siberian doggedness
Of the tall wood wolf that shrinks into its squint, and schemes.

Does baby take in anything? Will he understand better
Why, in his story book, the Town fled the Happy Lion?
The elephant and the rhinoceros were too big for him —
He simply gazed at their muddy sides as he does at landscape.
Only a llama calf alarmed him of all the animals,
Because as he stroked its breast its neck did a U turn
And sniffed the top of his head, hard.

Three weeks later, penned behind railback chairs,
A dead-pan polar bear cub rocks on prodigious muscles,
With a hint of razor-sharp menace in his expressionless mouth,
The wolf-scheme in his eyes, and even the puzzled frown of the tiger.

I remember a television interview,
The 'Jim Conway morning show,' Chicago:
'What kind of a man do you think did this murder?'
The girl's father answering this impertinence:
'Brother – you tell me!'

# GALACTICS

'There's a skyful of stars for my baby!'

You hold him, balancing on the windowsill
Craning up at the frosty November night.
After only six hundred days in the atmosphere
He can receive and exclaim about faint night light
Which began its journey before our galaxy was formed.

Here the waves beat on the new jelly of his eyes:
One of his first words is 'star'.
For him they merge with phantasy: subjective objects
No more nor no less real than the 'nasty man' in his dreams,
Or the way he behaves at times as if his mouth didn't belong to him:
When he feeds his sister's black doll he puts its hand in his mouth.

We try to follow Sir Bernard Lovell and Narlikar,
But shade off into quasars and quantum theory:
We are glad to find doubts over the meaning of the Red Shift,
And that the never-ending ends of the universe confuse them too.

There it all is, there's no doubt: I find some joy
In discovering at last that my experience of the sun
Is primary, while the astronomers are but trying to describe theirs.
So, the image of today is the huge red ball we saw
Against which black Newnham Hill lifted with alarming speed:
We exist in the stream of its solar winds,
Shielded only by the unseen magnetism of the Van Allen Zones.

A little warmth and colour comes to us on the Butts Road,
Touching in a consummateness on one of those soft Sundays
When we are moony, and your eyes go smoky.

Between the nadir and zenith of the sinking disc
I reviewed a thousand solemn settings like it:
In our Leicester apple tree, the Western Islands,
Across the Hampstead Ponds, and here behind the poplars:
Each fireball falling eats our quantum speck away.

On my desk is a coin: Imp. Otho Caesar . . . Pot.
Nero went off with his wife, Popaea Sabina:
Since the coin was minted there have been 700,000 sunsets.

I try the nought-game on various astronomical distances,
And try to imagine space being convertible into time:
On the Cambridge Road, the Mullard dishes confront them, the vacancies.
Thomas's view is more comfortable: he can do cosmic magic:
'Twinkle twinkle little moon!'

I feel like the old Woman tossed up in a basket,
Yearning to be in bed again, finding my centre
In your warm clasp, where I can forget that the earth wobbles,
That the astronomers can explain less and less,
And that even the blue sky is a mere light effect
Caused by irregular densities in almost nothing.

## ECCE HOMO

Suddenly, in the middle of the floor,
Without holding on to anything,
There you are, standing up!
Startled, we all cheer and clap round you: 'clever!'

You stare at us as if we were mad,
Gingerly bend your knees, then brace them:
Just my natural human posture, your face says.
But then you catch on, and clap your hands too,
Sit down with a bump, too hard, and cry a little.

So, you make the great transition:
You are an upright man.
Just for a moment this time:
Soon it will seem primitive to you to crawl.

Imagine the tall noisy individuals you call 'Man!'
Going on all fours down the street!
Such nonchalant pride to join us,
You with your pale hair and face clear as an angel's.
Bare puppy buttocks quivering with pride!

We'll try not to let you down.

Eventually we shall need to lead you to the discovery
How it is possible to be both upright and abject:
Or like you, wavering at first stance,
But without an audience to cheer:
The inward primitive, shakily taking to the attitude of the body,
Hardly daring to explore the perspective around it,
As the slow-learning psyche joins the body, so much of a life-time after
This first elevation to the two-legged assertion.

# UPSTARTS

The cattle bridge, made of railway sleepers,
Is soft and slimy with rot, over the stream.
Some of the crumbling beams have fallen:
There is no trace of them. The stream chuckles.

Twenty years under the railway, thirty on our bridge.
Now the wild roses and raspberry canes take root in them.
Some of them are already furry leafmould.
Thomas drops twigs through their rotten eyeholes,
Squeals as these swirl away down the sunlit spring water.

I am inert with overwork: my stiff legs stumble
On the greasy timber that rickets under me.
Another spring intensifies in the Valentine morning sun:
There is a frisson of scuttling everywhere:
A monotonous whistle call has been turning on itself all day.

'More waterfalling!' cries the baby.
Four times I have nabbed him in mid-air.
Lurching, I am suddenly transfixed by what comes into focus:
On the rail-bar, too flaky to lean upon,
A keen green cushion of fine star-spiked moss,
No bigger than a finger-palp, and married into it,
Blue lichen flowers like hollow tissue-spills,
Yearning towards me, frail as Alpine crocuses.

I jump to the other side of the bridge to grab my cub:
Only a pale smudge on the cracked bridge rail!

In focus, structures intensely alive to their season:
A yard away, a rot-smear on insignificant stuff!

'Come on, baby', I say, 'Let's find somewhere safer!'
The old bridge seems to mutter: 'Who do they think they are?'

## DEAD DUCK

A rotary motorscythe is an instrument of magic:
It eats the grass like hate.
Hate hits back in dank weather:
A tall wet blade shorts the spark circuit,
A cough, and the snarl's earthed:
The bruised silence sneers –
A two-stroke is a devil to re-start hot.

I curse the long grass after a damp September.
The battered blue chopper snags on molehills;
Each jolt judders the clutch-catch into my thumb;
The starter cord breaks and I scream obscenities at it;
Sweat drops fall on the rusty grass-box as I heave away.
The impeller chops windfalls; children's gew-gaws
I am sick of picking up I deliberately suck in;
Wood quoits, slashed sorbo, thunder into its throat;
I am the Leveller, no mere chore's idiot:
But the pose does not relieve my mow-ricked back.

In the tough water-grass, whoa! A crouched black back of feathers!
Immobile as the men on Green Beach: sod you, mow over it.
The loud scythe steers for the coot's corpse.
A hint stir of maggots deflects me:
I fear the sickly corpse smell that makes you puke:
I shrink the blade-slashed elbow bones and bits of slung guts:
A decapitated frog once pulsated like a red and green purse trying to run.

The damned machine won't stop: the clutch has gone:
Up and down I'm dragged, flanking the bird.
It lies in a mound of twitch and clover, a pearly dew-decked grave:
One white feather trimming the black, the underedges seeping.

Among the unmowable edges, its quick short life!
Black furball first like wind on the water only, subwing,
Then after innumerable circlings among the gnats,
Running its own strip of streamside,
A quick beak for territory, the little quick mutters of unseen matings:
Who notices the small windfall shadows scuttle back to the cress?

I found another in the orchard, more like loam.
What kills them? There were live coots, scuttling for safety.
But it was the dead ones that followed me indoors
Long after the vortex was silent. Most die unnoticed.
I probably never saw that coot alive: did no one.
Its tail flicked in the sunshine of three seasons,
Then it sank into the grass. The meta-questions
I would not have escaped by mowing up the remains;
Nor do I answer them by leaving them undisturbed —
A small still tussock disfiguring my lawn.

# GOING TO A WEDDING AFTER GATHERING WATERCRESS

The best times come as free as watercress.
I finger out the crisp wet March-green thongs
Where the stream inlets thickly foster it.

So long our loud geese and that scissoring swan
Wasted this water: now the pelt thrives again.
I squat and nip my shoots from hairy tendons.

It was once wasted off by those predatory birds
Supposed to glide as if chased in crystal
Across the middle distance. Instead they'd squat
Filthying up the doorstep with what remained of our watercress
After the best of it had become swan.

A poetic image would tap assertively on the door for scraps.

During one of our uglier quarrels
I rushed out and kicked it
Slithering in swan-shit I sat in the mess
Reflecting on the hypocrisy of idealising.

The stupid swan the watercress became
And the now swamping swanless watercress
Are in my mind all through a village wedding.
The unfortunate plumages and the drab penguin-suits:
The bride as a super-duck, with a decoy beside her.
Assertions of a mystical union: tips for a happy married life.
I want to shout, 'No swan-shit!'
                                        Who'd understand me?

By chance I touch your thigh, slim in a grey suit:
I dream of an idle moment, where the sun is on the cress-beds.
The free March gift of its growth!

                           One can only come upon it
Like the cress comes: hidden where the spring purls
The hairy roots under the flow of man and woman
Which either strike and shoot and yield a sap-green crop,
Or else are wasted away by the assertive maw.

May I come easy upon your cressbed soon!

I am glad to revert to the marquee.
How appropriate are my symbols?
The bridesmaids carry jonquil, and conifer,
Threaded with what looks like parsley:
So, why not watercress?

I wish I could say to the bride receiving her guests
In a bitter field wind of our hawthorn winter,
'The best times come as free as watercress!'

# ON THE BRINK OF A PIT

We had heard so much about Melanie already:
Couldn't eat our kind of food, our Saturday her Sabbath,
Went on Friday to say her prayers, was learning Hebrew.

I took our child to her party, carrying a book-token
Covered in child-gay seals, because they love one another,
And Melanie is saving to buy her great Jewish Bible.

The Sunday afternoon was full of the first bird-chimes of spring:
Warm sun honeyed the suburban gardens, and handsome women
Tapped over a few skeleton leaves on the muddy pavements.

Dimpled, graceful, dark-haired, a puppyish twelve,
Melanie assured me with guileless big blue eyes
Her father would bring Kate home, fondly drew her into the house.

I was suddenly overwhelmed: yet uninvolved,
A fountain of tears rose in me, misting the afternoon:
I wanted a thousand lives to worship what Melanie was —
No more than a pretty child. But all the previous night
I had wrestled with black perceptions: we are dead for ever:
We do not mourn the time before we came: being is all that matters.
Melanie's eyes my daughter loves were everything possible.

So I stood weeping unashamedly in the street in Letchworth,
There being as much hate in garden cities as at Maidenek,
Remembering a blurred photograph in a Polish book —

A handsome mother, like the ones who stare at me,
Clutching a child to her breast, like Melanie,
On the brink of a pit, and a storm-trooper aiming.

## AFTER TEACHING POETRY

The last short stretch of lane:
I am home again, under the familiar elms.
Pretty white wildflower lines each verge.
I am almost complacent about my interpretations:
I believe I have learned so much from the young men and women,
Discussing poetry in the sunlit college room.
Cambridge stone fades as I buck through the farmland:
Now the village church greets me through the poplars.
I stretch myself on the seat like a stubborn contented cat.

Above a gatepost in the lane rise two sinewy thongs
Like thin green adders' snouts, twisted together
In a knotted artery screw, rearing into the evening
As if with rabid fangs. The frowsty post is strangled,
Hopelessly skeined up in the death-whorls from the hedge.
That arrogant twist! The vicious speed of the creeper!
Already swagged, the hawthorn is sickly with its doom:
This anaconda weed has wound this since this morning!

Shaken, I lock the car without satisfaction:
My suavity is spoiled: I remember a dream of death,
A death thirst in the night: and you beside me
Lying as if dead, with your poor mouth open.
Only Old Man's Beard.'

The hedges cover themselves with it every summer:
Its fluffy flower, pale green, then faintly lilac white.
The finger of each thong screws into the world of May
As if to overwhelm with the vigour of that impetus
That first thrust tendrils out of sun-warmed mud.

I want an explanation: but the throttled gatepost
Suffers in cords that wind and grow themselves
Beyond the world of explanation — that one day they'll overwhelm.

The body I live in grasps as blindly at survival:
Within the body strips of molecules thus
Could garrot me as slickly in a growing month.

The creeper-points confound me all next day:
They twine like lathe-cut screws, menacingly regular.
How common stuff can grow so baffles me,
But neither can I make it a satisfactory symbol.
I fear it will slither across the meadow and drive me mad.
What stops it?

How far away my confident hour in class!

## DICHTERLIEBE

The young man sings with such rich exactness
From the whitewashed chancel in the sun:
The German poet is breaking his heart with idealism.
The singer's woman looks on, slim and beautiful.

*Ich liebe du!* It is real between them:
They hold hands with such excitement afterwards.

Wonderful thrilling songs! Gone with the last humming wire.
Heine's grief buried in a monstrous coffin, he said.

At home again, I read you the words of the songs in the sun,
Then cut them up with scissors to amuse the baby.
As we walk in the long grass you place my hand on your breast:
The garden is transformed into a green arena of expectancy.
I recall the music strumming on, the declamation,
The bitter sadness. Somehow they never met,
Poet and woman. Worse, say the stone skulls on the wall:
The wretched woman was no more than a screen,
The poet's plaintive anguish kneels at his own projections:
'O split-off self, I love you, you are so pure.'
So plangent, the exquisite art of self-torment.

At the end of his charming interpretation
The young man turns to brown skin and long fair hair:
I walk in the dampening long grass, aware of your moving thighs:

Poor Heine can go and bury himself and his self-defeating lies!

## THE FLIES

Heavy and humid July:
Everywhere today the flies madden;
Whining into the small horn of my ear
Persistently they follow my smell,
Hunting for eye-ducts and films of sweat.
They make me feel disgusting:
If I do not brush them away they will sip at the crack of my lips.

Pestered in a soggy corner of a meadow
I see them spray out in showers as I walk,
My feet clogged by the thick damp tussocks:
I flick and snort in that other animal dimension,
Flies' meat, smelly earth badger, weary old head-shaking bull.

I struggle to think of a subject, an issue:
Moving my hand in the study on working days,
I erect a pure and flyless world of paper,
And it seems to belong to a world of meaning,
With a secure perspective of time, of sequence and causality,
Such as a biological study of flies could have.

Down by the wood there is no history, nor histology.
There is only the dank moment, the flies biting,
The frantic itching and flaps that inhibit thought,
The pointless chasm of mere breathing existence,
Body and flies at odds, dark hints of night and breaking storm.

The flies follow me up to the house: as I look round
They hover behind, in my aura: do they wail at the door?
The squealing housemartins whirl about devouring them.
In my vengeance I transform them into an idea:
But outside the air is still thick with them,
A world dying under the eternity of the fly.

## NEVER FAR AWAY

*To the memory of Richard Hutt*

The garden descends in stages from the house:
A paved terrace where we drink coffee:
This year the roses are rotten, but beneath them
Small deep red Alpine strawberries, splashed with mud.

The lawn below is mown, but by the streamside
Stormwater stands on it still, and from the hedges
Advance thick self-sown wild rose thongs that claw:
The Japonica is strangled with convolvulus.

Turning the corner by the stream I enter the helpless orchard,
Given over now to gross marsh-grass and knotted couch.
Gale-tossed elm-limbs crush the nettle-beds;
Half a split willow lumbers across the mill-pool.

There the woodpecker scratches at his dead pierced perch;
In the overwhelming ivy hoods flutter the hidden pigeons.
Heavy July dew thickens, the light goes dead and gray,
And here the brink is never far away.

The flies bite as if one's flesh were dead,
And the maddening wild things sting and rip:
Down to the wood here's only a sodden step,
But here we come down to the spring stream's mud-choked bed.

Where the college lawns are cut three times three ways
And the lobelia is as regular as the tidy cobbles
I found it impossible to hear that one of my students
With whom I discussed half-a-dozen poems, was dead.

14

Here I can understand what has happened:
A cold sweat comes over me with the humid sunset:
I see his doubting face, as we talked about death —
And the concept of being glad that one had existed.

Did he have a moment in the Jugoslav river
To achieve the tragic view? Our exchanges mean nothing to buried flesh.
The one young man's death that I hardly knew
Lessens our whole security among the rain-crippled roses:
Greater my fears for my woman's illness-hollowed eyes:
As my children chase each other down the garden
They seem to be plashing down towards this brink,
Never far away. In the orchard alone I am able to think,
Yes, we are all making our way down to the wild place,
Where the water goes over for ever: you can hear it always down there,
Never far away, below the smooth lawns, never far away.

## MY FATHER'S GAY FUNERAL

This year has been a spoiler:
I have never seen so many rosebuds ruined
Never to unfold, the stained bundles perish,
Thud clammily under the straggling bushes.

A few fine days have proved to be transient,
Hustled ridges of air pressed by the next depression.

One of these housed his funeral: flowers everywhere
Lapping and sipping the late summer sunlight
With their pendent purple tongues and their eager scarlet faces,
Field of gay dahlias and thick crowded beddings,
Waves of hot honey with the bees scouring them.

Weep as we could, his coffin sailed vivid and gay
Through the September noon, lurched through the archway
Where he stood ten years ago to be photographed
After his second wedding: wreath-roses flipped the stone,
The air filled with torn blossom because we were late,
The air tearing garlands from his roof:
How he would have laughed!

                              Veiled, his widow,
After the Blessing snaps a rose from the cross,
Her hand on the ridge of the long box:
Then we go out, crying bitterly, among the sun-warm flowers.

But through our tears the massed petals under the walnut trees
Dance and are sparkling gay. So we comfort one another,
Riding back in the sun, leaving the last of that man
We loved in our different ways, in a bewildered exhilaration,
And we talk about fields where he played and flowery gardens.

Overnight, the rain returns: then the first autumn gale.
Soiled and sodden the flowers outside in the darkness.
The winds whirl the vapours of his pale bony body
Into the chaos of an icy ominous night:
Urgent, the dripping swallows assemble on the lines:
Our night thoughts dig to the real death truth.

But uppermost in the memory, in the mind's eye of him,
Is the man as a spoiled flower, all there filled
By the past bloom of him, the blossom dust we gathered,
As I saw gather bees from the plump grapes on a market stall,
On that same vivid day, when everything I saw
Spoke stubbornly not of trouble, but of the petals of the man.